produced by
MOTOR

C000183913

ROSS & RACHEL

by James Fritz

The first performance of *Ross & Rachel* took place on 6 August 2015 in the Assembly George Square Theatre, The Box, as part of the Edinburgh Festival Fringe 2015.

The show then transferred to the 2016 Brits Off Broadway Festival at 59e59 Theaters in New York and Battersea Arts Centre in London before embarking on a UK tour.

ROSS & RACHEL
by James Fritz

Cast   Molly Vevers

Creative Team
Director   Thomas Martin
Designer   Alison Neighbour
Production Manager   Nick Slater
Lighting Designer   Douglas Green
Sound Designer   Jon McLeod
Producer   Andrew Hughes (MOTOR)
Production Manager   Simeon Miller
(for original Edinburgh run)
Sound Associate   Bethany Taylor
(for original Edinburgh run)
Production Assistant   Andrey Khrzhanovskiy
(for original Edinburgh run)

Ross & Rachel has been generously supported by:
The Peggy Ramsay Foundation
The Really Useful Group Foundation
The Stage One Bursary Scheme for New Producers
English Touring Theatre Forge Scheme
Old Vic New Voices
The 2016 UK tour of *Ross & Rachel* is supported using public funding
by Arts Council England

The company would like to thank Katie Sherrard, Luke Thompson,
Sarah Schoenbeck, Emily May Smith and Kate Lamb for their time
and talent during the development of *Ross & Rachel*.

Cover art by Guy J Sanders (www.guyjsanders.com)

Biographies

Molly Vevers

For *Ross & Rachel* Molly was awarded The Stage Award for Acting
Excellence 2015. Molly trained at the Royal Conservatoire of Scotland
(formerly RSAMD). Upon graduating, Molly won the Highly Commended
Spotlight Prize 2012 and went on to work with Dundee Rep ensemble as
their graduate actor. Theatre credits include an extensive tour of *An Ideal
Husband* as Mabel Chiltern (Ash Productions Live); *A First World Problem*
(Theatre503); *How to Build a Better Tulip* (Tabard); *The Sleeping Beauties*
(Sherman Cymru); *Kora* (Magnetic North/Dundee Rep); *Time and the
Conways* (Royal Lyceum/ Dundee Rep); *The Snow Queen, She Town* (Dundee
Rep). TV credits include *Doors Open* (ITV/Sprout Pictures). Radio credits
include *The Legend of the Holyrood Vampires, School Run, Maldinis* (BBC
Radio/The Comedy Unit), *Much Ado About Music* (BBC Radio 3).

James Fritz (Writer)

James Fritz's first full-length play *Four Minutes Twelve Seconds*, was runner-up
of the Soho Theatre's 2013 Verity Bargate Award. It premiered at Hampstead
Theatre downstairs in 2014 and was nominated for an Olivier Award for
Outstanding Achievement in an Affiliate Theatre before transferring to
Trafalgar Studios in 2015. It then won him the Most Promising Playwright
prize at the Critics' Circle Theatre Award 2015. His play *Parliament Square*
won a Bruntwood Prize in 2015. He is currently writing new plays for
Hampstead Theatre and the National Youth Theatre, and is working on a
comedy-drama series for Leftbank Film and Television. He is the recipient of
a 2016 residency at the BANFF playwrights Colony in Canada, and will also
be on attachment to the National Theatre in 2016.

Thomas Martin (Director)

Thomas Martin is a London-based theatre-maker, working across directing,
writing, performance and live art. Aside from developing *Ross & Rachel*, he
recently directed *Followers*, Stewart Melton's adaptation of Shakespeare's
Julius Caesar, at Southwark Playhouse. In 2011 he directed James Fritz's
debut play *Lines*, and was a finalist for the JMK Award. He has shown work
across the country, at venues including BAC, New Wolsey, Forest Fringe
and Cambridge Junction, and runs the feted videogames-and-performance
night *Beta Public* at CPT. www.thomasjamesmartin.co.uk

Alison Neighbour (Designer)

Alison is a designer for theatre, events, installations, and film. She trained at RADA following a Masters degree in English, Writing & Performance at the University of York. She makes theatre that sets out to challenge and provoke, and is interested in creating performance in unusual spaces, bringing the unexpected into everyday environments. Alison is also founder and co-artistic director of Bread & Goose, a company who create engaging journeys for audiences, through collaborative working practices and a design-led approach. The company's production of *The Incurable Imagination of Anthony Jones* was performed at the World Stage Design Festival 2013 and selected for inclusion in the 2015 Make/Believe exhibition.

Recent design work includes *The Curtain* (Young Vic); *Derailed* (BAC/HOME, Manchester); *Colour* (Libraries tour); *Funny Peculiar* (UK tour); *This Room* (UK tour); *Roland: A Collage* (Bikeshed, Exeter); *Lost in the Neuron Forest* (UK tour); *Crazy Gary's Mobile Disco* (Chapter Arts Centre/Welsh tour); *Phenomenal People* (Camden People's Theatre/ARC, Stockton/Colchester Art Exchange); *I Told You This Would Happen* (ARC Stockton/UK tour); *Spine* (Underbelly/Soho; Fringe First & Herald Angel winner); *Square Bubble* (National Theatre: Watch This Space); *The Eyes Have It* (Imagine Watford); *Wedding* (Shoreditch Town Hall); *The Literary Ball* (L'institut Francais); *Spectra* (mac, Birmingham); *Romeo & Juliet: Unzipped* (Salisbury Playhouse); *Followers* (Southwark Playhouse); *Used Blood Junkyard* (Arcola); *Late in the Day* (Hen & Chickens); *A Conversation* (UK tour); *Le Peau du Chagrin* (Holland Park); *Harmless Creatures* (Hull Truck). For Bread & Goose, site-based work includes *Return* (Dunraven Bay); *Siege* (Shoreditch Town Hall); *The Eyes Have It* (Watford Town Centre); *Lost in the Neuron Forest* (UK tour); *Stations By Heart* (St Pancras Station); *Mission: A Stranger's Promise* (Camden People's Theatre); *Mission: It Has Begun* (Scarborough Town Centre); *Fox in the Snow* (Brixton Market). www.alisonneighbourdesign.com

Nick Slater (Production Manager)

Nick has worked as a freelance production manager since 2013. His various projects include national tours of *Early Days (of a Better Nation)* (Coney – Annette Mees); *Shh!* (C-12 Dance) and *The Disappearance of Sadie Jones* (Hannah Silva). His London work includes *The Cocktail Party* (The Print Room) and *Electric* (Big House). Between 2013–2015, Nick worked with the Young Vic Theatre's Taking Part Department, making work alongside professional creative teams, community groups and young people. His work there includes *The Sound of Yellow* (Matthew Xia), *The Beauty Project* (Kirsty Housley), *The Surplus* (Jonathon O'Boyle), *All Stones, All Sides* (Finn Beams) and *Now Is the Time To Say Nothing* (Caroline Williams). The final production of these toured to the Edinburgh Fringe Festival, Forest Fringe Festival and Shabbat Festival in 2016. Other work at the Young Vic includes technical support for *Golem* (1927); *Staging a Revolution* (Belerus Free Theatre); and *If You Kiss Me, Kiss Me* (Young Vic); and production management of youth 'parallel' productions: *The Cherry Orchard* (Anthony Lau), and *A Streetcar Named Desire* (Rebecca Frecknall).

Douglas Green (Lighting Designer)

Douglas lives and works as a lighting designer in New York City.

Theatre includes *Chef* (Soho/Latitude Festival); Theatre Uncut 2014, *The Bread and the Beer* (Soho/UK tours); *Step Live* (Sadler's Wells); *A New Play for the General Election, Laburnum Grove* (Finborough); *The Dreamer Examines His Pillow* (Old Red Lion); *Opera in the Gardens* (Chiswick House); *SOLD* (Pleasance Forth); *Songs for a New World* (Bridewell); *Sweeney Todd* (Rose).

Fashion and corporate theatre include: Vivienne Westwood Red Label, Richard Nicoll, and Gieves and Hawkes (London Fashion Week). With Imagination: Rolls Royce Closed Room Tour, and Launch of RR6 (Private residence in Beverly Hills and world tour), Global Launch of the Jaguar XE (London Eye/the Thames), Land Rover Discovery Sport Gobal Debut (The Seine, Paris), and booths and launches for various automotive brands at the New York, Los Angeles, Toronto, Detroit, Washington DC, Brussels, Paris, Moscow, Delhi, Kingdom of Saudi Arabia, Shanghai, Beijing and Busan International Motor Shows.

As Associate/Assistant: *Don Giovani, Don Quixote* (Royal Opera House); *Privacy, The Physicists* (Donmar Warehouse); *4000 Miles* (Bath Theatre Royal).

Douglas trained at the Royal Central School of Speech and Drama. www.douglasgreendesign.co.uk

Jon McLeod (Sound Designer)

Credits include *A Conversation, Party Skills for the End of the World* (Nigel Barrett and Louise Mari); *In the Neuron Forest, The Eyes Have It* (Bread & Goose); *Spine* (Soho); *Arthur's World* (Bush); *The Fanny Hill Project, Tribute Acts* (TheatreState); *Free Fall* (The Pleasance); *Nightmare Dreamer, Flying Roast Goose, The Boy in Darkness* (Blue Elephant); *Borderline Vultures* (The Lowry); *Heartbreak Hotel* (The Jetty); *66 Minutes in Damascus* (LIFT Festival); *Made in Britain* (Old Red Lion); *The Invisible Show* (RedShift Theatre).

Andrew Hughes (Producer)

MOTOR is the producing partnership of Andrew Hughes and Jenny Pearce. Andrew is a 2015 recipient of the Stage One Bursary for new producers and is currently Assistant to the Artistic Director at the Young Vic Theatre, London. He began his career with Punchdrunk and has previously worked with Vicky Graham Productions, Siobhan Davies Dance and Blind Summit. www.producedbymotor.co.uk

ROSS & RACHEL

James Fritz

Acknowledgements

Thuli and Em, who helped us find out what the hell this was.

Emily, who has been very patient.

And Andrew and Tom, who have helped build this thing from the ground up. This play is as much by them as it is me.

J.F.

For Dad, who was nothing like this

Note on Play

This is a play with two voices for one performer.

The performer should use their own accent.

This text went to press before the end of rehearsals and so may differ slightly from the play as performed.

Sometimes, I just get really fucking sick of it. Don't you?

No.

Never?
No.
I've always loved it I don't know why you'd
It's nothing to do with you it's just
What?
Don't worry about it.
What?
Don't give me that look I said don't worry about it.
I'm not looking like anything.
It's nothing to do with us I just don't like people thinking we come as a package.
We do come as a package.
Like we're the same person or
We're a team
Right but
They see us as a team. That's a good thing.
Right, I know but.
I see us as a team don't you see us as a team?
Right yeah of course but when somebody emails you something that's meant for both of us, I don't see why they can't just email me as well.
It's just easier that way.
But it's always you. They always email you, but address it to the both of us.
You're worried about emails?
Forget it.
No go on.
It's fine.
I want to understand.
It's just. I don't know when people started saying our names together. You know? I don't know when that happened.

We are together.
Yes, but, I mean. Why do they always have to say my name
second?

Happy birthday to you happy birthday to
Thank you
Thank you
Thank you for coming
We're so pleased you could make it.
Forty-five. I know, I know.
You don't look it. Tell her she doesn't look it.
Stop it. You're embarrassing them.
Hey so glad to see you.
You guys make the cutest couple we were just saying weren't
we honey?
We were, yeah.
How long have you two been together now? You've still got
that look about you.
Did you ever hear how we first met? Right from the first
moment I saw her, standing next to my sister, I knew.
Not now, honey.
Strap yourselves in, you're not gonna believe this story.
They don't want to hear about that.
You guys think that's good? Tell them about how we got back
together. She tells it better than I can.
No, I don't.
Of course you do!
Let's just enjoy
Tell them! Isn't that the most romantic story?
She's perfect. She's a prom queen and I'm a nerd.
Honey
She's a prom queen and she belongs to me. Doesn't that make
you feel great about the world?
Let's talk about something else.
Tell them about the time we
Not. Now.
Tell them.
Tell them.
Tell them!

Right from the first moment I saw her, standing next to my sister, I knew.

Don't look at me like that.
I would never cheat on him.
It's not anything serious, Daniel's just a friend from work that's all.
Okay, so we held hands in the office kitchen. Briefly. But it wasn't even a

I am so lucky to have her. When she walks through the door every evening I still get that feeling you know? Just like. Wow. She's mine, you know?
That woman belongs to me and I can't believe my luck.

But I've been staying at work longer and longer and then I come home to.
I come home to him and it's just. You know. It's not *bad* but.

I can't do it. I can't have this argument again.
It's not an argument it's a discussion.
It's my job. What do you want me to do?
Leave on time. I manage it.
Your job is different to mine.
Less important?
Nothing's changed.
What do you mean?
This is the same argument we were having in our twenties and you remember how that turned out.
Oh I wondered when you were going to bring that up. We were on a –
Don't say it. Do not say it. If you say that word I swear I will walk out that door.
I wasn't going to. Look at me. I wasn't. Listen, I'm sorry, I just want to spend some time together that's all.

True love.
That's what our relationship is.

It's not that I regret it, exactly.

People always say that without really meaning it don't they.
But that's what it is.

I mean we were on again off again on again off again for so
long. Well you know. You were there.

It's like, I have to know what she's doing, all the time, just so
I can picture her doing it, I can feel close to her or. I'll be like,
'Hey, what are you doing?' and she'll text back like, 'I'm at
work' or 'I'm at lunch with so-and-so' and then I'm like 'Okay!'
and I just feel better.
Sometimes I'll just show up at her work and take her to lunch.
Just surprise her, you know?

I feel guilty talking to you like this. Things aren't so bad really.

So where shall we go?
I don't know honey. Somewhere close by. I'm very busy.
I know this new place that you're gonna love.
Is it a long walk? It's just I've got to get back to the office.
Wait.
Honey? Did you hear me? Is it a long walk because I promised
Bill that I'd.
Wait. I feel. F F
What?
F-for
What's the matter?
F-for for for f f
Oh my god. What's wrong? Honey? Your face it's all
For out out out t t t
Oh my god.
T t t t t t
Oh my god help us please please somebody help him somebody
help him!

We're getting married!

What time is it?

We're getting married!

God damn my neck is sore. There's a stain on the hospital curtains.

We're getting married again in the place where we had our first date because an unexpected catastrophe struck our original venue.
All our friends from down the years are in attendance.

Don't wake him up.

My best friend is the best man and my other best friend is conducting the ceremony.

Which way is the bathroom? Thank you.
God. I look awful.

I'm nervous because a series of unlikely events has delayed the bride's arrival and I'm starting to worry she's not going to show.

He's tossing and turning.
Always sleeps funny in a strange bed.
Jesus. It's so fucking hot in here.

The music starts, and comically mismatched pairs of my family and friends walk down the aisle.
Everything is perfectly positioned.

Really need to get some sleep.

The music changes and there's a gasp as she walks in looking more beautiful than I have ever seen her.
As she reaches me, I tell her she is my Princess Leia.
Everybody awws.

There is a mix-up with the vows. Everybody laughs.
And then it's done. And then we kiss and we kiss and cheering cheering from the audience.

Everybody is so happy for us and they turn to each other and they say thank god they finally did it. We've been waiting for this wedding for years. The whole world has been waiting for this wedding for years.

She tosses the bouquet and the bridesmaids all tackle each other and then the crowd parts and somebody unexpected is holding it and it's the funniest thing we've ever seen.

Our first dance in the place where we had our first date, and the stars are shining above us, and our beautiful children are there, my daughter is so tall and my son is with his girlfriend and we're married again and suddenly we're on the stairs of the Titanic *and we're kissing and all our old friends from the boat are bursting into applause and then*

Where am I?

Are you okay honey?
Didn't mean to wake you.

I can feel it in my brain. It itches.

Ten minutes until our meeting with the consultant.
He'll tell me that the tumour in my brain is benign. Right?
That's what he's going to tell me.
Of course that's what he's going to tell me.

That elevator came a bit quickly didn't it and that doctor's door was closer to the elevator than I would have liked and oh look he's opened the door almost instantly and oh great we're inside.

No. Put it out of your head.
I didn't have to be in this room.
Not now.
The two chairs in the doctor's office are different colours.
Keep a straight face. I want her to think that I'm calm.
He looks terrified.

The doctor is still talking.
Oh fuck oh fuck oh positives oh fuck oh treatable oh fuck oh fuck oh plan of action.

I'm not going anywhere.
I'm not going anywhere.
I'm not going anywhere.

Just another morning. Just another morning.
Where's my dinosaur tie? You seen my dinosaur tie?
Have a nice day.
You too. Don't overdo it.
Don't worry. I've given this lecture a hundred times before.

Five minutes until lunch with Daniel. Maybe we'll go to that
Vietnamese place round the corner and I'll tell him what's going
on, and he'll hold my hand and he'll say oh no I'm so sorry are
you okay and then he'll say do you want to go for a walk and
he'll put his arm around me and he'll say it's going to be
alright. And maybe I'll look up at him and then we'll stop and
then he'll kiss me. And at first it's really tentative and then we
just sorta sink into it and at first his hands start on my waist and
then they come up and they're in my hair and
Sorry say that again I was miles away.

Maybe I should tell my students what I'm fighting. I'll make
a joke about it so that they'll all be impressed by my strength
in the face of adversity and they can smile at me in the
corridor and say how are you doing how are you feeling oh
I'm so sorry to hear oh Professor I was thinking of running a
half-marathon in your honour I was thinking of growing a
moustache for your cancer.

Daniel seems genuinely worried about me.
Thank you.
That hug lasted just a second too long.
Didn't it?
I'm sorry Daniel, I need to take this.

My phone has been going off all day. You told everyone?!
I thought they'd want to know.
On the fucking internet?
What's wrong with that?
Without even talking to me? And oh, surprise surprise, you've
signed it from both of us.
I couldn't have just put my name. It would have looked weird.
Read it. I said some really nice things about you.

Look at me. Hey. Look at me. I know you're worried. I'll be fine. Trust me. This isn't how this ends.

He's very strong.
She's my rock.
How you feeling?
CAT scan on Wednesday.
She's been great, you know.
We're just taking each day
We're getting through it you know
We're
We're
We're
Diet plan.
Medication charts.
How you feeling?
The consultant.
Pills.
Chemo.
Frontal lobe.
Radio.
Coffee?
He'd love to see you.
Swelling.
Steroids.
Thank you for the flowers.
I'm going to be sick.
Coffee?
Side effects.
Oh.
Coffee?
Juice?
Cream?
What time's the appointment?
D'you take sugar?
Oh.
So great to see you.
Thought they'd never leave.
Beer?

Coffee? Coffee? Coffee? Coffee? Coffee? Coffee? Coffee?
Coffee? Coffee? Coffee? Coffee? Coffee? Coffee? Coffee?
Coffee? Coffee? Coffee? Coffee? Coffee? Coffee? Coffee?
Coffee? Coffee? Coffee? Coffee? Coffee? Coffee? Coffee?
Coffee? Coffee? Coffee? Coffee? Coffee? Coffee? Coffee?
Coffee? Coffee? Coffee? Coffee? Coffee? Coffee? Coffee?
Coffee? Coffee? Coffee? Can I get you a coffee? Coffee?
Coffee? Coffee? Coffee? Coffee? Coffee? Coffee? Coffee?
Coffee? Coffee? Coffee? Coffee? Coffee? Coffee? Coffee?
Coffee? Coffee? Coffee? Coffee? Coffee? Coffee? Coffee?
Coffee? Coffee? Coffee? Coffee? Coffee? Coffee? Coffee?
Coffee? Coffee? Coffee? Coffee? Coffee? Coffee? Coffee?
Coffee? Coffee? Coffee? Coffee? Coffee? Coffee? Coffee?
Coffee? Coffee? Coffee? Coffee? Coffee? Coffee? Coffee?
Coffee? Coffee? Coffee? Coffee? Coffee?

Wait.
What.

Oh.

Up to a year.

I've
Got.
He.
Has.
Anywhere up to
Anywhere up to a year.
Are you okay?
I'm fine.
I'm fine.
I don't think he's fine.
I'm fine.
A year's a long time.
A year's a long time.
This is our end and it's.
It hits you like a bullet news like that. It hits you like a train and
I'm devastated that –

But actually. No.
You know what?
If I'm honest.
If I'm totally honest I feel. Deep down.
And this is just between us right?
I. Feel.
Because the thing about him, the thing that I forgot all those
years that we were broke up in our twenties and thirties. The
thing about him is he's actually really. Fucking. Boring. We
have nothing in common, is that horrible to say? I'm not sure
we ever did. Sometimes he talks to me and you know what?
I couldn't give less of a shit. No. No I don't mean that. Please
don't tell anyone I said that. I'm just. I'm just tired is all.

The thing about her is

He doesn't care about my work, about anything I'm interested
in, I just happened to be the first woman he got to know that
wasn't his fucking mom and then bam, here we are. He had
a crush on his sister's best friend and then somehow we both
ended up here, and I'm going through this and it's driving me
crazy it's driving me fucking crazy because this is not what
I had in mind for my forties let me tell you. I'm sorry I
shouldn't be saying this to you I'm just tired I'm just really
fucking tired.

She's mine. And I know that won't change. Even when I'm.
Right from the first moment I saw her, standing next to my
sister, I knew. She belonged to me.

When we first got back together I thought it was just a part of
getting used to each other again. But that feeling never went
away and now I've been on the brink of leaving for. But I don't.
I haven't left.
Because.
Because well, you know. It's me and him.

This is really boring.

I want to strike up a friendship with a sassy nurse who says something sassy at precisely the right moment to break the tension.

I want there to be mishap with my hospital gown that leaves me stranded naked in the corridor having to use a fire extinguisher to cover my genitals.

I want to look in the bed next to me and oh my god it's my high-school football coach who yells my last name and says get down and give me twenty.

I want her to put down her magazine and to take my hand and give me the speech that I hope she's going to give me where she tells me that she loves me and that we make the perfect team and we'll face this together and that our strength as a couple is more than a match for what's going on inside my body.

Wouldn't everybody love that?

I can't stop

Can't stop worrying about what she'll do when I'm gone.

This can't actually be the end for us. Can it?

You okay honey?

I'm fine.

Daniel! Oh my god.

That's hilarious.

Me, go to Australia, with him?

It's just a joke.

I can feel myself.

Just a joke.

Listen, I, and I don't know how to say this Daniel, it's a bit awkward really but I don't think we should spend time like this. Any more. And I know, I know we're just friends and it's not that I don't enjoy it but what with everything at home...

Oh. He gets it. He's not fighting me.

Thanks for being such a great friend, I knew you'd understand.

Look at all those couples.

Look at all those fucking couples out there.

Which one will leave. Which one will run. Which one is cheating on the other. Which one will die first. Him. Him. Her. Him.

Look at that girl there. She's what? Mid-twenties? Look at how she looks at him.

I was just her. Wasn't I? And now. How did that happen? I was
just her.
She has no fucking idea what's coming for her. None of them do.
Grab her. Tell her it's not going to turn out like that you young
fucking stupid fucking idiot it doesn't work that way. It's not
about hand-holding. It's not about first dates. It's not about will
they won't they or on again off again or he's the one or weddings
or new-baby smell or airport reconciliations and the people who
tell you it is are liars they are liars and they'll keep telling you it's
about all that but it's not. It's about everything in between.
Off she goes. Happy as a fucking songbird.

How are you feeling, honey?
Fine.
The least he deserves. To be there for him. That's what I'm for,
right? That's what I'm for.
Because he does love me. And I.
I said that I'd be there for him.
Fuck.
Did he just feel me recoil?

I can feel it
I can feel it inside my head it feels itchy feels like a scab like
a spider bite right here and so I reach into my pocket and I take
out my keys and I find the pointy one that opens our front door
and I stand in front of the mirror and I take a deep breath and
I open my eyes wide wide like this and I hold them open and
I take the point the point of the key and I go in behind the eye
through the side and it goes black and I start to dig, dig behind
the eye and I feel the squish and then I hit bone I hit bone at the
back of the socket. I keep gouging and I scratch scratch scratch
until I've made a hole in the bone and then I'm in and I can feel
it and I dig so hard and I get right in there and I scrape it out
I scrape it out of my head and I hold it in my hand a black lump
black dirty gristle and then I flush it I flush it and then

She's still asleep.
The keys on the bedside table.
Try to fall back to sleep.

Hi Daniel.
No, I
He's trying. At least he's still trying.
I can't I'm
Not tonight, maybe
All I want to say is

He's stopped trying.
He's not Daniel any more. He's just Daniel from work. Daniel
across the hall. Daniel who's dating Julie or Jessica. Daniel
who's moving back to Australia?
Oh. Great. That's exciting.
Home. Hiya. How you feeling?
Anywhere up to a year.
Up to a year.

He's coming up from LA.
Really? Why?
He wants to see you.
He looks fat.
You boys have fun. Don't let him drink too much.

TWO MORE PLEASE. BOURBON. I DON'T KNOW, WHAT
DO YOU HAVE? YEAH. YEAH THAT SOUNDS GOOD. IS
THAT GOOD?

THE BARMAN LOOKS LIKE A GOOD GUY. I WAS JUST
TELLING MY FRIEND, YOU LOOK LIKE A GOOD GUY!
AND HOW ARE YOU, BY THE WAY? THAT'S GOOD.
THAT'S GOOD. LONG SHIFT? ARE YOU WORKING A
LONG SHIFT?
LISTEN. WANNA KNOW SOMETHING? I HAVE CANCER.
NO NO, HE DOESN'T MIND, DO YOU? YOU DON'T MIND.
YOU CAN ASK MY DOCTOR YOU DON'T BELIEVE ME.
NO, NO, THAT'S NICE OF YOU TO SAY, THANK YOU.
THESE THINGS HAPPEN, YOU KNOW? THAT'S NICE.
THAT'S NICE OF YOU. HOW OLD ARE YOU MAN?
TWENTY? TWENTY-ONE?
I WAS TOP OF MY CLASS, DO YOU KNOW THAT? PHD.

I'M A *DOC-TOR*. NOT THAT THAT.
I'M GOING TO BE A HUGE LOSS TO MY FIELD.
THEY'LL WRITE THINGS ABOUT ME, YOU KNOW?

LISTEN TO ME. MY WIFE? SHE'S. SHE'S. SHE'S FUCKIN'
BEAUTIFUL, MAN. SHE IS. DO YOU WANT TO SEE? LET
ME. HERE. I'VE GOT A PHOTO. SHE'S. VERY.
SUPPORTIVE. SHE IS. I AM SO LUCKY TO HAVE HER.
BUT. NO.
HERE. LOOK AT THIS
ACTUALLY NO, NO WAIT. I HAVE A YOUNGER PHOTO.
HOLD ON.
HOLD ON!
HERE'S WHAT SHE LOOKED LIKE WHEN WE FIRST
GOT TOGETHER. SHE'S TWENTY-FIVE IN THAT
PICTURE. RIGHT? FUCKING SUPERMODEL RIGHT?
HE KNOWS. YOU TOTALLY WOULD, *RIGHT*? IF YOU
SAW THAT WALKING ROUND CAMPUS, YOU'D BE
NO, NO COME ON WE'RE JUST HAVING A
CONVERSATION.
BUT SHE KNOWS. SHE KNOWS WHAT SHE'S LOSING.
SHE WON THE FUCKING LOTTERY GETTING WITH ME,
YOU KNOW? BECAUSE SHE MIGHT BE BEAUTIFUL.
SHE MIGHT HAVE RICH FUCKING PARENTS BUT I'M A
FUCKING SMART
MAN. I'M A SMART, WHITE, SMART FUCKING MAN
WHO KNOWS HOW TO TAKE CARE OF HER, AND WHO
LOVES HER, AND I'VE FUCKING GOT MY SHIT
TOGETHER, AND, YOU KNOW, AND THAT'S, THAT'S
THE FUCKIN' GOLDEN TICKET WHEN IT COMES TO
TO
GOOD LUCK TRYIN' TO FIND ANOTHER ONE OF ME,
THAT'S WHAT I'M SAYING.
I FUCKIN' LOVE HER THOUGH. I DO. I DO. SHE WAS.
WE KNEW EACH OTHER AS TEENAGERS, DID YOU
KNOW THAT? SHE'S A PROM QUEEN AND SHE
BELONGS TO ME. DOESN'T THAT MAKE YOU FEEL
FUCKING
AND I CAN'T STOP PICTURING HER ALL ALONE

WITHOUT ME AND THAT MAKES ME SADDER THAN
ANYTHING.
WE GOT A KID, YOU KNOW THAT? WE GOT A
BEAUTIFUL LITTLE GIRL. SHE LOOKS JUST LIKE HER
MOM, SHE DOES. SHE'S GOT HER LOOKS AND MY
BRAINS. SHE'S GONNA BE SO BEAUTIFUL WHEN SHE
HOW OLD ARE YOU? TWENTY? TWENTY-ONE?

HEY!
TAXI! HEY!
AH. FUCK.
TAXI!!
Bed. Don't wake her up.
Don't. Wake. Her…

*I'm alone on the rooftop of the apartment I had when I was a
young woman and the sky full of stars is so bright that it hurts
my eyes to look at. I turn and I feel my hand being taken and
I'm whirled around the dance floor and when I look up I
realise that what I'm dancing with is a six-foot lobster. The
lobster spins me around and it won't let go and I see that the
stars are not the stars but actually the lights of the ceiling a
projection and we're lying on a picnic blanket and we're wet
we're soaked through actually because I just rolled over the
juice box. The lobster gets up and beckons only now I can't see
his face, and every time I try and get around to his front he gets
a little further away until he is outside in the rain oh god he's
outside and I'm trapped behind a glass door a glass door to a
coffee shop that has been bolted several times and it's raining
and he bangs his head upon the windowpane and he wants to
come in, he wants to come in, he*

I can feel it more and more.
Headaches and nausea and
And we're
I can taste metal in my mouth.
I'm so tired but I can't say anything.
His sense of smell is not
What will it be like?
What will it actually be like when it happens?

I want to ask but I don't ask.
Honey?
What is it actually going to feel like.
Honey are you?
I want to know. I want to know. I don't want to know. I want
to know.
Do I feel myself soften or
Honey are you feeling okay?
Will she tell me, will she tell me when I've got a week left?
A day left? An hour?
And what happens after?
What happens after it's done?

I have a picture of my life after he's gone.
I'll still live in our house.
I'll still see our friends.
I'll still raise our daughter.
And every day little things remind me that he used to be here
and now he's not.
Everything feels
For the first few months I can't move for visitors. They all want
to take me out for coffee.
And then that stops. They go back to their lives.
I'm left all alone and
And you know what.
I'm okay.
It's actually really great.
I miss him sometimes
But
It's horrible but I'm excited I'm actually a bit excited to find out
who I am when he's not around any more.
To live without an 'and' in front of my name.
I start making selfish decisions.
I start putting my job first again. And it works.
I become more successful than I could ever have imagined.
Because I love my job.
I've always loved my job.
And I'm good at it. I'm so fucking good at it. I have the time to
start my own business and it actually goes really well.

My daughter and I become closer than ever. She grows into a
better woman than I could have hoped.
I have dates and flings and they're fun and strange and not quite
But mostly, it's just me. And that's not because of anyone else,
it's not because of what our friends might say, it's not because
of loyalty.
It's because that's what I want.
And then, at some point, that changes. Maybe when my
daughter has gone off to college. Maybe before then.
I meet a kind, handsome man. Not Daniel from work. Maybe
Daniel from work.

I feel like I'm going to vomit. Oh.

It's strange to be with someone new but it's also exciting and he
talks to me in a way that I'd forgotten was even possible.
Eventually we move in together and when he proposes he does
it somewhere hot. Maybe we have a small wedding in the
spring and after the honeymoon we move to Paris where I've
always dreamed of working.

Whatever happens after you're gone, I promise I'll be happy.
Why did I just tell him that?
Why did she just tell me that?
Maybe I think it will make him feel better.
Maybe I think it will make him feel worse.

I want her to be happy. I want her to find somebody else.
And I know she will. Because she's still a young woman a
beautiful woman and that's how things go, isn't it?
She'll find someone else straight away and she'll spend many
years with him, maybe even more years than she spent with me.
And that's okay.
I know that maybe when she dies aged eighty it will be him that
talks at her funeral and I'll be referred to as her *first* husband.
And that's okay. That's fine. It will be him and not me who sees
our children, my children, who gets to know the people they
become. It will be him who holds my grandchild. Him who's
buried next to her.
Him who gets to be with her who gets to eat with her and walk
with her and sleep with her and kiss her and fuck her and and

hear her laugh and see her get old while I'm. I'm. What?
Nothing. Nowhere.
It will be him who becomes the love of her life and that is.
That is
That's absolutely fine.
Of course I want her to find someone else. She deserves it.
Of course.
Although.
Fuck her and whoever she finds. It's not right, it's not right, you
know, because this is, this is me and her. I hope she feels guilty.
I hope the guilt it chokes her. I hope whoever he is he treats her
like shit. I hope he beats her. I hope he treats her well. I hope he
cheats on her. I hope she's happy. I hope she's unhappy. I love
her so much.

Honey, are you okay?

I can picture it. Her and him her new husband and his hands his
hands all over her I want to be sick I want to be sick get off her
you asshole you fucking asshole she belongs to me she belongs
to me. She belongs. To. Me.
No. No. This can't be it, this isn't what was supposed to
happen. This is not the end of me and her.

He's hanging on in there. We're doing fine thanks for asking.
He's strong, so strong, you know? Except he's not strong. He's
boring.

But actually. Look at her.
Maybe it's okay. Maybe she's worried about the same thing.
How can she go on without me?
That's what she's thinking.
How can she go on without me?

I've got to get out of this house. I love him. We've got nothing
to say to each other. I can't remember the last time I talked
about television or politics or gossip or anything that wasn't to
do with –

Now that's an idea.
A way for this to end where
God, wouldn't that be –

Jesus Christ what's the matter with me.
Think about something else.

It's like he's given up.
No, Mom, he just sits there. He won't do anything. No I've
tried. I've tried talking to him, but you know what he's like.

Can't help coming back to the same idea.
Would she consider it? I could ask her.
Maybe…
Come on. Stop it. Get a fucking grip.

Come on honey.
Let's turn the TV off. Yeah? It's a beautiful day.
Let's take a walk.
Let's go for dinner.
Let's go for coffee.
Let's go and see your parents.
Let's go to the park.
Let's go to the movies.
Let's take a holiday.
Let's stay on a yacht.
Let's take a cruise.
Let's see the world.
Let's swim with dolphins.
Let's swim with some fucking dolphins! How about we just
take you out there and let's get you kitted up and let's throw you
in the sea with some smart fucking dolphins and you can swim
until your legs hurt and your eyes sting and the dolphins have
bruised you from nuzzling too hard and you're tired and the
dolphins are tired and let's get a photo of you in the water with
your thumb up honey, let's get a photo of the dolphin smiling
next to you and we can share it we can send it to your mum and
dad we can send it to all our friends and we can keep that, me
and the kids we can keep that for ever.
Let's do a bungee jump.
Let's do a fucking bungee jump, how about that? Honey, eh?
How about we do. That.
Let's turn the TV off. Yeah?

Let's take a walk.
Okay. What are we watching?

Can't stop thinking about it.
I wonder. I couldn't ask her. I could never ask her. Could I?
But maybe. Maybe
What better way to end things?

Thank you so much for stopping by. He's not at his best
today but.
How are the twins?
Coffee? Beer?
Come in. Sit down. We're watching TV.

It's not like it hasn't happened before.
The Japanese even have a word for it.

Thank you so much for coming.
Some days are better than others. He gets confused.

I know what her answer will be. I know what her answer will be
and I'm terrified but I'm excited.
Everyone has always hated seeing her with someone else.
Everyone hates it when she's alone.
They'll understand.
They know what this relationship means. To us. To everyone.
I'll talk to her tonight.

He looks tired. His face looks odd. I'll have another glass
of wine.
Take her hand.
He's taken my hand.
Do you love me?
Do I love him?
Of course.
Of course, she says!
Something's not right.
Completely?
Of course, what's up? Don't blink.
You do. I know you do.
He's shaking.

Is everything alright? Do you need me to call someone?
When the time comes
Oh god.
When I get too ill, I've decided that I want to finish things
myself.
This isn't a surprise.
Okay. Okay. If you want to, if that's really what you want,
we can talk about it. We can talk about how.
He's smiling.

I've been thinking and, and I really think that this could be,
could be a really beautiful thing. I've been thinking what if,
what if, what if you did it too?
What if I did what too honey?
That smile.
Wait.
He can't mean
He doesn't mean?
I want you to do it too.
I
I want us to do it
Together.
What do you think?
I I
It's what everyone wants.

She looks me in the eye and she says
She says yeah. I will do that with you.
Of course I will because we're one really, aren't we?
She's just a girl, standing in front of a boy. She completes me.
To me, she is perfect.
And now I can't believe this is happening. I can't believe that
this is what we're going to do. They'll think we're mad. They
will write that it's a terrible tragedy for two young parents to
take their life. They will write that it's a terrible tragedy for a
beautiful young woman like her to take her life.
But it's not a terrible tragedy. This is the perfect end to our
story. And that's been obvious right from the start.
We sit down at the kitchen table to talk through the specifics.

She takes my hand in hers and says to me honey, this is all I've ever wanted. You and me. Together for ever.

We talk about when and we talk about where. We talk about who we're going to tell and how we're going to say goodbye. We talk about what music we will play and what clothes we will wear. We talk about the lighting.

We're getting everything in order as if we were planning a wedding. We've told my sister, and she is being very supportive. She has even made a to-do list because that's what my sister does.

I'm excited but I'm terrified but I'm excited.

We write out a note to the kids and a second note to our friends that is full of references to jokes we made in our youth.

Everybody laughs a sad laugh. Hand in hand we go upstairs and we prepare to run our bath. The one with the perfect ending.

She is looking into my eyes as the bath begins to fill.

We say

We say the things that we were always meant to say.

We fill it right to the brim. Not so it spills.

And then, before she gets in we kiss. We kiss a kiss that has the audience on their feet.

It's always been you.

As she lowers herself into the bath she looks more beautiful than ever. I say she is my Princess Leia. Everybody laughs. Everybody sighs.

I pass her the razor and she smiles a sad smile a happy smile. I show her where to make the incision. Right here. The music starts. A short gasp and then

As the water turns red in slow motion I hold her hand. I hold her hand. It's okay, I say. It's okay. It's okay.

And then it's my turn and I hold the razor and I count to three and

The perfect ending. Everyone is waiting to applaud.

One.

Two.

What if I did what too honey?

That smile.

Wait.
He can't mean
He doesn't mean?
I want you to do it too.
I
I want us to do it
Together.
What do you think?
I I
It's what everyone wants.

He's joking. Of course he's joking.
He hasn't made a joke in months but still, he must be joking.
But.
His eyes. His mouth.
He isn't.
Oh god, he isn't joking.

Calm down, honey, you're confused.
You're not thinking straight.
That's far too tight.

Look him in the eye.
Look him in the eye and say
No.
No!
Of course not. Of course I can't do that. Won't do that. Ever.
Ever ever ever.
That's just
Mad.
Fucking madness.

To think of me
To be so
And your children your fucking children.
Get off me.
Please.
Ow that hurts that fucking hurts.
Please.

Get off me.
Please!
GET OFF!
Thank god.
I didn't know what he was going to do. I didn't know what he
was going to do.

Hello? Yes he's had, had some sort of turn or. Well I don't
know, he won't stop, won't stop sobbing. He grabbed me and.
Please come quickly.
Look at him.
I can't be here.
To ask me that.
I'll wait for the ambulance to come and I'll tell them what
happened and while they are talking to him I'll walk out
that door.
I'll go to my mom's house. God.
What am I going to tell her.

I can't sit still.
I feel terrible.
I feel sick.
And meanwhile he is
He is
For the first time since I can remember I don't know how
he's doing.
What's the matter with me?
I shouldn't have left him like that.

I am still so angry with him.
But his room is horrible.
The view from his window is of a wall.
And he looks.
His face looks.

Do you want me to change the channel? Did you hear me
honey? Do you want me to change the channel?
You can go in.
He's on a lot of morphine so he might not
Honey? Look who's come to see you.
I won't tell anyone what he asked me. I don't think I ever will.

Hi Mom.
No, no he's not in any pain because of the
God I'm tired. I'm so fucking tired.

The things he did to me when we were young the time he spied
on me the time he wrote those things or his constant jealousy or
the time he cheated on me with that girl from the that girl from
the why now why am I thinking about that now it's been years.
Stop it stop it stop it.
What's the matter with me? Try and focus on the good things.
How he kissed me when.
It's my birthday and, and he's bought me
The girl the girl from the what's the matter with me the girl the
girl the fights what's the matter with me what he asked me
every last cruel word he ever said to me stop it stop it.
He hasn't woken at all this morning.
Coffee?

The doctor says he can still hear me.
Should say something to him before
A speech, or
I can't. Or. I don't want to.
I really don't want to.

What's the time?
His face.
I think. I think his breathing's changed.

Honey? Can you hear me?

As she lowers herself into the bath she looks more beautiful than ever. I say she is my Princess Leia. Everybody laughs. Everybody sighs.
I pass her the razor and she smiles a sad smile a happy smile. I show her where to make the incision. Right here. The music starts. A short gasp and then
As the water turns red in slow motion I hold her hand. I hold her hand. It's okay, I say. It's okay. It's okay.
And then it's my turn and I hold the razor and I count to three and
The perfect ending. Everyone is waiting to applaud.
One.
Two.

My eyes.

The bath?
Where where am I oh no oh no.

Shh.

She's still here she's still here where am I?

Shh. It's okay. I'm here. His eyes.

No I don't want this. I don't want this.

It's okay honey. His eyes are open. Should his

I can hear you.

I'm just going to. I'll be back in a minute honey I'm just going to go get someone.

Where did you go? Fuck you where did you go you fucking bitch come back come back.

This is it.
I think this might be it.
In a moment it will just be

me.
His eyes are open, he's very restless, is there anything you can
give him?

Please.
I'm thirsty. Who. I can see.

What do you want? What can I get you? I don't know what
he wants.

Please.
Don't stay.

Can't you give him something?
Thank you. His breathing.

My eyes.
Get off.
Hold me.
Where am I.
What hurts.
My eyes.
Don't stay.
I'm thirsty.
Who said.
What time.
Who said that.

It's okay. It's just me here. Me and you.

My throat.
I don't.
Her face.
My house.
What time.
I'm thirsty.

How old.
Why this.
Air.
What's that.
Where are.

It's okay. I'm here.

Don't let me.
Water.
Hello.
Help.
Where is she.
Don't let me.
No one told me.
What is.
Where is.
Water. Water.
My mouth.
I am.
What's happening.
What's.
No one told me.
No one told me.
No one told me.
No no no
No no.

Please.

I'm thirsty.
I'm.

I think that's it.

It's just me.

Oh.

I'm the only one here.

Other Titles in this Series

Mike Bartlett
BULL
GAME
AN INTERVENTION
KING CHARLES III
WILD

Tom Basden
THE CROCODILE
HOLES
JOSEPH K
THERE IS A WAR

Jez Butterworth
JERUSALEM
JEZ BUTTERWORTH PLAYS: ONE
MOJO
THE NIGHT HERON
PARLOUR SONG
THE RIVER
THE WINTERLING

Caryl Churchill
BLUE HEART
CHURCHILL PLAYS: THREE
CHURCHILL PLAYS: FOUR
CHURCHILL: SHORTS
CLOUD NINE
DING DONG THE WICKED
A DREAM PLAY *after* Strindberg
DRUNK ENOUGH TO SAY
    I LOVE YOU?
ESCAPED ALONE
FAR AWAY
HERE WE GO
HOTEL
ICECREAM
LIGHT SHINING IN
    BUCKINGHAMSHIRE
LOVE AND INFORMATION
MAD FOREST
A NUMBER
SEVEN JEWISH CHILDREN
THE SKRIKER
THIS IS A CHAIR
THYESTES *after* Seneca
TRAPS

Phil Davies
FIREBIRD

debbie tucker green
BORN BAD
DIRTY BUTTERFLY
HANG
NUT
RANDOM
STONING MARY
TRADE & GENERATIONS
TRUTH AND RECONCILIATION

Vicky Jones
THE ONE

Anna Jordan
CHICKEN SHOP
FREAK
YEN

Lucy Kirkwood
BEAUTY AND THE BEAST
    with Katie Mitchell
BLOODY WIMMIN
CHIMERICA
HEDDA *after* Ibsen
IT FELT EMPTY WHEN THE
    HEART WENT AT FIRST BUT
    IT IS ALRIGHT NOW
NSFW
TINDERBOX

Cordelia Lynn
LELA & CO.

Conor McPherson
DUBLIN CAROL
McPHERSON PLAYS: ONE
McPHERSON PLAYS: TWO
McPHERSON PLAYS: THREE
THE NIGHT ALIVE
PORT AUTHORITY
THE SEAFARER
SHINING CITY
THE VEIL
THE WEIR

Jack Thorne
2ND MAY 1997
BUNNY
BURYING YOUR BROTHER IN THE
    PAVEMENT
HOPE
JACK THORNE PLAYS: ONE
LET THE RIGHT ONE IN
    after John Ajvide Lindqvist
MYDIDAE
THE SOLID LIFE OF SUGAR WATER
STACY & FANNY AND FAGGOT
WHEN YOU CURE ME

Phoebe Waller-Bridge
FLEABAG

Enda Walsh
BALLYTURK
BEDBOUND & MISTERMAN
DELIRIUM
DISCO PIGS & SUCKING DUBLIN
ENDA WALSH PLAYS: ONE
ENDA WALSH PLAYS: TWO
MISTERMAN
THE NEW ELECTRIC BALLROOM
ONCE
PENELOPE
ROALD DAHL'S THE TWITS
THE SMALL THINGS
THE WALWORTH FARCE

A Nick Hern Book

Ross & Rachel first published in Great Britain as a paperback original in 2015 by Nick Hern Books Limited, The Glasshouse, 49a Goldhawk Road, London W12 8QP, in association with MOTOR

Reprinted with revisions 2016

Ross & Rachel copyright © 2015, 2016 James Fritz

James Fritz has asserted his right to be identified as the author of this work

Cover art by Guy J Sanders (www.guyjsanders.com)

Designed and typeset by Nick Hern Books, London
Printed in Great Britain by CPI Group (UK) Ltd

A CIP catalogue record for this book is available from the British Library

ISBN 978 1 84842 522 4

CAUTION   All rights whatsoever in this play are strictly reserved. Requests to reproduce the text in whole or in part should be addressed to the publisher.

Amateur Performing Rights   Applications for performance, including readings and excerpts, by amateurs in the English language should be addressed to the Performing Rights Manager, Nick Hern Books, The Glasshouse, 49a Goldhawk Road, London W12 8QP, *tel* +44 (0)20 8749 4953, *email* rights@nickhernbooks.co.uk, except as follows:

Australia: Dominie Drama, 8 Cross Street, Brookvale 2100, *tel* (2) 9938 8686, *fax* (2) 9938 8695, *email* drama@dominie.com.au

New Zealand: Play Bureau, PO Box 9013, St Clair, Dunedin 9047, *tel* (3) 455 9959, *email* info@playbureau.com

South Africa: DALRO (pty) Ltd, PO Box 31627, 2017 Braamfontein, *tel* (11) 712 8000, *fax* (11) 403 9094, *email* theatricals@dalro.co.za

United States and Canada: Berlin Associates, as below

Professional Performing Rights   Applications for performance by professionals in any medium and in any language throughout the world should be addressed to Berlin Associates, 7 Tyers Gate, London SE1 3HX, *fax* +44 (0)20 7632 5296, *email* agents@berlinassociates.com

No performance of any kind may be given unless a licence has been obtained. Applications should be made before rehearsals begin. Publication of this play does not necessarily indicate its availability for performance.

MIX
Paper from
responsible sources
FSC® C013604